AF510018

Table of Contents

1 Introduction to Refugee Law

The 1951 Refugee Convention, along with its 1967 Protocol, forms the cornerstone of international refugee law. These instruments define a refugee as someone who, owing to a well-founded fear of being persecuted for reasons of race, religion, nationality, membership of a particular social group, or political opinion, is outside the country of their nationality and is unable, or owing to such fear, is unwilling to avail themselves of the protection of that country. This definition, while seemingly straightforward, has been subject to extensive interpretation and debate over the years, leading to complex legal challenges in its application. The core principle underpinning the Convention is non-refoulement, prohibiting the return of a refugee to a place where they face a serious risk of persecution. This fundamental principle is widely considered a cornerstone of international human rights law, reflecting a global commitment to protecting vulnerable individuals. However, the practical application of non-refoulement often presents significant challenges, particularly in situations of mass displacement or where states have limited capacity to provide adequate protection. Understanding this central concept is crucial for anyone navigating the complexities of refugee law.

States that ratify the Refugee Convention undertake specific legal obligations. They must refrain from returning refugees to places of danger and, in many cases, grant them at least temporary protection. The extent of these obligations, however, varies depending on the specific treaty provisions and national laws. Some countries have incorporated the Convention's provisions directly into their domestic legislation, creating detailed procedures and legal frameworks for refugee status determination. Others have a more ad hoc approach, relying on case-by-case assessments and less formal processes. The level of protection provided also differs considerably. Some states offer comprehensive social services and integration programs for refugees, while others provide only basic assistance and limited rights. The differing levels of commitment highlight the inherent complexities in international cooperation on refugee protection.

The process of seeking asylum is often fraught with challenges and uncertainties. Applicants often face lengthy administrative procedures, bureaucratic hurdles, and lengthy delays. Many have to navigate the process without legal representation, exacerbating the difficulties they face. The burden of proof generally rests with the asylum seeker to demonstrate a well-founded fear of persecution, requiring them to provide credible evidence to support their claim. This can be particularly difficult for individuals who have fled situations marked by violence and instability, lacking the documentation necessary to substantiate their accounts. The standards of evidence needed often vary across jurisdictions, leading to inconsistencies in the outcomes of asylum applications. The assessment process frequently involves detailed scrutiny of an individual's personal history, requiring them to recount traumatic experiences and relive past suffering.

National legal frameworks addressing refugee status determination often reflect broader immigration policies and political considerations. Asylum laws frequently interact with national security concerns, with individuals from countries deemed to pose a security threat often subjected to stricter scrutiny. The integration of refugee populations is another area where national policies play a significant role. While some states focus on fostering social inclusion, others adopt more restrictive approaches, limiting access to services and opportunities. These differing approaches illustrate the wide range of political, social, and economic factors influencing how countries approach refugee protection. It is crucial to analyze the interaction of refugee law with broader domestic policies to gain a nuanced understanding of its practical implementation.

Understanding refugee law requires a detailed knowledge of international and national legal frameworks. It's essential to grasp both the theoretical foundations of refugee protection and the practical realities of asylum procedures. Navigating the intricate legal landscape of refugee protection demands close attention to detail, thorough research, and awareness of the cultural and political context in which these laws are applied. This is further complicated by the evolving nature of refugee flows, driven by ongoing global conflicts and crises. Staying current with developments in international refugee law is crucial for those working in this field, as new challenges and interpretations continually emerge, necessitating adaptation and the development of new strategies for protecting vulnerable populations. The legal field concerning refugees is complex and requires continuous learning.

1.1 Defining Refugee Status

The 1951 Refugee Convention, supplemented by the 1967 Protocol, forms the cornerstone of international refugee law. This foundational document defines a refugee as someone with a well-founded fear of being persecuted for reasons of race, religion, nationality, membership of a particular social group, or political opinion, and who is unable or unwilling to avail themselves of the protection of their country of nationality, owing to such fear. Crucially, this definition hinges on the concept of persecution, which requires a level of severity exceeding mere discrimination or hardship. It necessitates a demonstrable threat to life or freedom, a threshold demanding careful consideration in individual cases. The interpretation of "well-founded fear" also proves complex and often litigated, necessitating a careful balancing act between ensuring genuine protection and preventing fraudulent claims. This demands a nuanced understanding of the specific context surrounding each case, acknowledging the unique realities and vulnerabilities faced by individual asylum seekers.

States party to the Convention bear distinct obligations, paramount among which is the principle of non-refoulement. This fundamental principle prohibits the return of a refugee to a place where they face a real risk of persecution. Non-refoulement is a jus cogens norm, implying it holds absolute and overriding force in international law. Violations are considered grave breaches of international human rights law, attracting both international condemnation and potential legal challenges. However, ensuring the effective implementation of non-refoulement presents numerous practical challenges, ranging from identifying genuine refugees amidst a large number of applicants to handling situations where a safe third country might theoretically exist. Such practical complexities regularly test the limits of the legal framework, demanding careful consideration of human rights considerations when navigating legal ambiguities.

The definition isn't static; its interpretation evolves through jurisprudence and changing political contexts. For instance, the concept of a "particular social group" has been significantly debated, with legal precedent constantly refining its scope. Cases involving sexual orientation, gender identity, and other marginalized groups illustrate the dynamism of the refugee definition. Courts and tribunals frequently grapple with defining the boundaries of this crucial aspect of the refugee definition, often producing detailed analyses of the nuances of social identity and the nature of the threat faced by asylum seekers. The evolving understanding of human rights and the multifaceted nature of persecution ensure that the concept of refugee status remains a consistently evolving and complex legal domain.

Furthermore, proving refugee status often relies heavily on evidence. Asylum seekers must provide credible accounts of their experiences, often using documentation like witness statements, medical records, and media reports. However, obtaining such evidence can be particularly difficult for those fleeing persecution, especially considering the urgency of their circumstances. Their safety may depend on the quick processing of their application, which further adds to the pressure. The burden of proof often becomes an issue, highlighting the ethical need for a fair and comprehensive assessment of each individual claim, requiring sensitivity to the trauma potentially experienced by those seeking asylum.

The process of determining refugee status is inherently complex, involving careful analysis of individual circumstances within a broader legal framework. It necessitates meticulous examination of evidence, rigorous legal reasoning, and careful consideration of human rights. The subjective nature of "fear" and "persecution" highlights the crucial role of impartial adjudication, demanding independent bodies and robust legal processes. The practical application of the legal definition consistently tests the limits of international and national legal systems. The challenges of applying these general principles to specific situations demand ongoing consideration and reform within national legal systems. The success of the refugee protection system relies on effective implementation of international law, ensuring fair and humane treatment for all. The pursuit of justice for refugees requires a constant reevaluation and adjustment of processes to meet the varying challenges of refugee applications.

1.2 International Legal Frameworks

The 1951 Refugee Convention, the cornerstone of international refugee law, defines a refugee and outlines the obligations of signatory states. Crucially, it establishes the principle of non-refoulement, prohibiting the return of a refugee to a place where they face a well-founded fear of persecution. This principle, though seemingly straightforward, is often complex in practice, requiring careful interpretation and application, particularly in situations involving multiple countries and overlapping jurisdictions. Its strength lies in its universality, yet its weakness stems from the varying levels of commitment and implementation by different nation-states. The 1967 Protocol extended the Convention's geographical scope, addressing the limitations of its original focus on post-World War II Europe. This expansion was a crucial step in ensuring broader protection for refugees globally, reflecting the evolving nature of displacement and conflict worldwide. However, the Protocol's success hinges on consistent, global application, a challenge given the diverse socio-political contexts in which refugee flows occur.

The UNHCR, the UN High Commissioner for Refugees, plays a vital role in overseeing the implementation of the Convention and providing international protection to refugees. Its mandate includes assisting states in fulfilling their obligations, providing humanitarian aid, and advocating for refugee rights. The UNHCR's work is often crucial in situations where national systems are overwhelmed or inadequate, serving as a critical bridge between international law and on-the-ground realities. The agency's influence, however, depends heavily on the funding it receives and the political will of nation-states to cooperate. Challenges include navigating complex political landscapes, securing funding and resources in times of widespread crisis, and addressing the often conflicting interests of states and refugees themselves. Their actions are constrained by the limitations inherent in relying upon the cooperation of sovereign nations.

Beyond the Refugee Convention, other international and regional instruments contribute to the legal framework surrounding refugee protection. These include human rights treaties, such as the Universal Declaration of Human Rights and the International Covenant on Civil and Political Rights, which provide further protections for refugees' fundamental rights. Regional agreements, like the African Charter on Human and Peoples' Rights and the Cartagena Declaration, reflect specific regional challenges and approaches. These supplementary agreements offer additional layers of protection but sometimes also introduce complexities arising from differing interpretations and enforcement mechanisms, creating inconsistencies in the application of refugee law across jurisdictions. Their effectiveness depends on effective domestic implementation, and, as such, varies significantly.

Understanding the intricacies of these international frameworks is essential for practitioners and policymakers working with refugees. The legal landscape is constantly evolving, with new challenges arising from factors such as climate change, armed conflict, and global migration patterns. Furthermore, the interpretation and application of these legal instruments often require careful consideration of national laws and the unique contexts in which refugee claims are made. Navigating this complex legal terrain requires specialized knowledge, including a deep understanding of international human rights law, refugee law, and domestic immigration regulations of the relevant jurisdictions. The practical implications for determining eligibility and access to protections, particularly concerning the definition of persecution and the assessment of well-founded fears, can be extremely complex and often nuanced.

The interplay between international and national laws is crucial. While international law provides a framework, states retain considerable discretion in implementing its provisions. This can lead to disparities in the treatment of refugees, depending on national legislation, policies, and administrative practices. A key area requiring careful attention lies in harmonizing international obligations with domestic legal systems. This often necessitates a multifaceted approach involving both legislative reforms and administrative adjustments, encompassing training, capacity building for decision-makers and immigration officials, and the establishment of efficient and equitable asylum procedures. The aim is always to create a system that is both legally sound and practically effective in protecting the rights of asylum seekers. The inconsistencies across national implementations often undermine the overall effectiveness of the international legal system, leading to inequalities in access to protection and often resulting in a global imbalance in the distribution of refugees.

2 Asylum Procedures in Europe

The Dublin Regulation, the cornerstone of the EU's asylum system, aims to determine which member state is responsible for examining an asylum application. Its core principle is that the application should be processed in the first EU country the applicant entered. While designed to prevent "asylum shopping," the Dublin system has faced substantial criticism. Its implementation often leads to lengthy transfers between countries, leaving asylum seekers in limbo and vulnerable to exploitation. The system struggles to cope with large-scale influxes, exacerbating existing pressures on overburdened national systems. Furthermore, the uneven application of the Dublin Regulation across member states creates significant disparities in asylum procedures and outcomes, raising serious concerns about fairness and the principle of equal treatment for all asylum seekers regardless of their entry point. The lack of sufficient solidarity mechanisms among member states further undermines the effectiveness of the Dublin system.

National asylum procedures within the EU vary significantly, reflecting differing legal traditions, political priorities, and administrative capacities. Some countries have streamlined procedures with relatively short processing times, while others face protracted backlogs, resulting in lengthy delays and uncertainty for asylum seekers. The criteria for assessing asylum claims can also vary, leading to inconsistencies in outcomes. Reception conditions, including housing, healthcare, and access to legal assistance, differ considerably across member states, raising concerns about the quality of support provided to asylum seekers and their ability to access justice. These variations not only challenge the fundamental principle of equal treatment but also contribute to unequal access to protection and potential violations of human rights. Moreover, the differing approaches taken by national authorities highlight the complex interplay between national sovereignty and the EU's commitment to providing unified protection for those seeking asylum.

The European asylum system faces numerous challenges. The ongoing migration crisis has placed immense strain on national asylum systems, leading to unprecedented backlogs and processing delays. Furthermore, the rise of anti-immigrant sentiment and xenophobia in several EU member states has created a hostile environment for asylum seekers, eroding public support for refugee protection. The system's struggle to accommodate the increasing number of asylum applications has raised questions about its long-term sustainability. A lack of coordinated action by EU member states is exacerbating this issue. Internal conflicts within the EU, particularly regarding the sharing of responsibility for asylum seekers and the management of external borders, further complicate the process and compromise its effectiveness. Addressing these challenges requires a holistic approach that encompasses greater cooperation between member states, investment in improved processing capacity, and efforts to combat xenophobia and promote a more inclusive societal attitude towards refugees.

Reform of the European asylum system is crucial. Many proposals advocate for a more equitable distribution of responsibility among member states, possibly through a quota system or other mechanisms that promote solidarity. Strengthening the EU's external border management to prevent irregular migration is another key component of proposed reforms. However, this must be done in compliance with international human rights law. Improved information sharing and cooperation between national authorities could streamline procedures and reduce inconsistencies in asylum decision-making. Investing in legal aid and support services for asylum seekers is also vital to ensure that they have adequate access to justice and can effectively present their cases. Furthermore, ongoing monitoring and evaluation of the asylum system's performance are necessary to identify areas for improvement and ensure that the system operates in accordance with international human rights standards and the principles of fairness and due process. A fundamental shift in the political discourse surrounding asylum is necessary, one which emphasizes empathy, understanding, and commitment to upholding the rights of those seeking protection. Only through such comprehensive reforms can the European Union hope to build a more just, efficient, and humane asylum system.

2.1 The Dublin Regulation

The Dublin Regulation, a cornerstone of the European Union's Common European Asylum System (CEAS), aims to determine which member state is responsible for examining an asylum application. Its core principle is to prevent asylum seekers from "asylum shopping"—submitting applications in multiple countries, hoping to find a more favorable outcome. The regulation designates a single member state responsible for processing each application, based primarily on the first point of entry into the EU. However, the system's complexity and its inherent reliance on effective cooperation between member states have proven to be significant challenges.

While the intent behind the Dublin Regulation—efficient and fair processing of asylum claims—is laudable, its implementation has been fraught with difficulties. The system often places an undue burden on frontline states, those geographically closest to external borders, which receive a disproportionate number of asylum applications. This uneven distribution has led to criticisms of unfairness and strain on national resources, creating a logistical nightmare for these nations. Furthermore, the practical realities of determining the first entry point, particularly in cases involving irregular migration, are often problematic.

The regulation's deficiencies became particularly evident during the 2015 migrant crisis, when the influx of asylum seekers overwhelmed many member states' capacities. This exposed fundamental flaws within the system, demonstrating its inability to cope with large-scale migration movements. The mass movement of individuals across borders, often aided by human trafficking networks, further complicated efforts to identify the point of first entry. This led to protracted legal battles and delays in the processing of asylum claims, often leaving vulnerable individuals in a state of limbo for extended periods. The regulation's emphasis on first entry point also disregards the realities of asylum seekers' journeys, frequently forcing them to return to countries where they faced danger or persecution.

One of the regulation's most significant shortcomings is its lack of flexibility. The rigid framework fails to account for exceptional circumstances, such as cases of family reunification or the presence of particularly vulnerable individuals who may require specific support and processing in a different member state due to prior family ties or pre-existing conditions. The system's inability to adapt to individual needs often results in separation of families and the exposure of vulnerable individuals to further harm. This inherent rigidity has been a major subject of criticism, prompting calls for a more nuanced and humane approach to determining responsibility for asylum applications.

Furthermore, the regulation's reliance on effective inter-state cooperation is unfortunately often undermined by a lack of political will and resources among member states. The practical challenges of transferring asylum seekers between countries, including logistical arrangements and ensuring their safety and well-being during the transfer process, have posed significant hurdles. This has led to delays in processing applications and, in some cases, failures to comply with the regulation's provisions. This failure has a direct and damaging consequence; it undermines trust and cooperation within the

CEAS.
Over the years, several attempts have been made to reform the Dublin Regulation. The most notable include the proposed reform of the Dublin system, which aimed to create a fairer and more sustainable mechanism for allocating responsibility for asylum applications among the member states. However, these efforts have often been met with significant political resistance, largely rooted in concerns about national sovereignty and the distribution of responsibility. Therefore, the current system remains a subject of ongoing debate and reform efforts, striving for a balance between efficient processing and the protection of vulnerable individuals' rights.
The Dublin Regulation's strengths and weaknesses underscore the complexities of managing asylum claims within a supranational framework. While it aims to prevent asylum shopping and create a more orderly system, its inflexible application and reliance on full cooperation between member states have significantly hindered its effectiveness. Continued efforts to reform the regulation, to increase flexibility and foster a more humanitarian approach, are essential to ensure a just and efficient asylum system for all within the European Union. Addressing logistical challenges, promoting genuine cooperation, and improving protection for vulnerable individuals must lie at the heart of future reforms, ensuring a system that is both efficient and respects the inherent dignity of all asylum seekers. It's a system constantly requiring re-evaluation and adaptation to meet the ever-evolving challenges of migration. The fundamental need for a humanitarian and legally sound approach remains paramount.

2.2 National Variations

Significant disparities exist in the application of asylum law across Europe, despite the existence of the Dublin Regulation. Germany, for instance, often prioritizes family reunification and offers more comprehensive integration programs compared to countries like Greece, where reception conditions are frequently criticized by human rights organizations and asylum seekers face protracted delays in processing their claims. These discrepancies lead to uneven protection standards and create incentives for asylum seekers to move within the EU, thereby overburdening some member states while others remain relatively less impacted. The resulting "asylum shopping" undermines the very principle of a unified European asylum system.

Consider the contrasting approaches to defining "well-founded fear of persecution." Some countries adopt a stricter interpretation, demanding demonstrably concrete evidence of past persecution or a credible threat of future harm. Others, recognizing the inherent difficulties in providing such evidence, particularly for those fleeing state-sponsored violence or organized crime, opt for a more flexible, holistic assessment, considering the totality of circumstances and the individual's vulnerability. This divergence in interpretation directly influences the success rate of asylum applications and underscores the significant impact national legal interpretations have on individual outcomes.

Furthermore, access to legal assistance plays a crucial role in determining asylum success rates. While some countries offer comprehensive legal aid programs, guaranteeing representation to all asylum seekers regardless of their financial means, others rely on a patchwork of pro bono services and limited public funding, resulting in significant disparities in access to justice. Consequently, individuals without adequate legal representation are often at a disadvantage, lacking the expertise necessary to effectively navigate complex legal procedures and present a compelling case for their asylum claim. This disparity underscores the need for consistent and equitable access to legal counsel as a fundamental principle of a fair asylum system.

Processing times also vary drastically across European nations. While some countries process applications relatively swiftly, within a matter of months, others are plagued by massive backlogs, leaving asylum seekers in protracted limbo for years, often experiencing significant psychological distress and social isolation. These extended delays can exacerbate the vulnerabilities of asylum seekers, as their legal status and access to essential services remain uncertain. This can ultimately affect their integration prospects, making long-term resettlement considerably more difficult. Efficiency in processing is therefore crucial for effective and humane asylum systems.

The interaction between national laws and EU directives further complicates the picture. The Dublin Regulation, aiming to determine the responsible member state for processing an asylum application, has been widely criticized for its shortcomings and its potential for leading to human rights abuses. Its implementation varies across member states, with differing levels of compliance and enforcement. This inconsistent implementation, alongside the ongoing challenges of managing irregular migration flows across borders, necessitates a re-evaluation of the system's effectiveness and the need for substantial reforms to ensure fair and efficient processing of asylum applications while also protecting the rights of vulnerable individuals.

National cultural perspectives and public opinion also shape the political landscape of asylum procedures. Countries with a history of accepting refugees and a generally welcoming attitude towards immigrants often adopt more inclusive policies, while others, influenced by factors such as national identity and security concerns, may implement more restrictive measures, resulting in significant variations in policy and practice. Understanding these diverse social and political factors is vital in comprehending the nuances of asylum processing within different national contexts. A holistic approach is needed, that addresses both the legal and socio-political elements influencing refugee protection in Europe.

Finally, the resources allocated to asylum systems vary greatly, influencing both the quality of services provided and the overall efficiency of the process. Countries with adequate funding can invest in comprehensive reception facilities, provide essential services like healthcare and language training, and ensure sufficient staffing levels to handle a large volume of applications, leading to improved outcomes for asylum seekers. In contrast, underfunded systems often struggle to cope with the demands, leading to inadequate reception conditions, delays in processing, and an overall diminished quality of protection. This resource disparity therefore presents a significant challenge to achieving equitable standards of asylum protection across Europe. The unequal distribution of resources and the resulting variability in reception conditions and processing efficiency underscore the need for greater solidarity among European nations in supporting asylum systems.

2.3 Challenges and Reform

The Dublin Regulation, designed to streamline asylum applications within the EU, has instead created a complex and often unfair system. Its reliance on the first country of entry principle frequently leaves vulnerable individuals trapped in countries ill-equipped to handle their needs. This has led to significant backlogs, inadequate reception conditions, and prolonged uncertainty for asylum seekers, forcing many to navigate bureaucratic labyrinths alone, far from their home countries and support networks. The system's inherent flaws, coupled with diverging national interpretations, render consistent application of the Regulation elusive. The result is a fragmented and inefficient system, riddled with inconsistencies and lacking in a genuinely unified approach. This creates a sense of legal limbo for those seeking protection, undermining the very principles of the European Union's commitment to human rights. Furthermore, the practical challenges of implementing the Dublin Regulation are exacerbated by the reality of irregular migration flows and the uneven distribution of asylum seekers across member states, leading to tensions between individual nations and creating an unsustainable situation for the asylum system as a whole.

National variations in asylum procedures across Europe paint a stark picture of uneven protection. While some countries boast relatively efficient and well-resourced systems, others are overwhelmed, leading to long processing times and inadequate access to legal aid. This disparity creates a situation where the outcome of an asylum application can depend heavily on the country in which it is filed, a clear injustice that undermines the principle of equal treatment under the law. The inconsistencies extend beyond processing times; standards of accommodation and access to essential services, including healthcare and education, vary significantly across the EU, leaving asylum seekers in precarious situations and perpetuating inequalities based purely on geography. The lack of harmonization in legal frameworks, procedures, and standards creates a system vulnerable to exploitation and abuse, offering varying levels of protection and leaving individuals subject to the whims of differing national interpretations and capacities. This lack of uniformity is a fundamental obstacle to creating a truly effective and humane asylum system in Europe.

Reform efforts within the European asylum system are critically important, but progress remains slow and uneven. While the EU has undertaken various initiatives to address the challenges, significant hurdles remain. The ongoing debate over burden-sharing amongst member states highlights the deep-seated political disagreements that impede effective reform. Moreover, practical obstacles, such as capacity limitations and resource constraints in many countries, continue to hamstring progress. Further complicating matters is the need to balance the protection of refugee rights with the concerns of national security and public opinion. Striking this balance requires careful political navigation and a willingness to confront difficult policy choices. Genuine progress requires addressing the underlying causes of the problems, rather than simply implementing superficial adjustments. Addressing the root issues necessitates not only legislative changes but also a fundamental shift in perspectives across Europe, fostering a culture of solidarity and shared responsibility for protecting those fleeing persecution.

The human cost of these systemic failures is immeasurable. Many asylum seekers endure protracted periods of uncertainty, living in substandard conditions, and facing significant challenges in accessing basic necessities. The psychological toll of navigating complex bureaucratic processes while dealing with the trauma of displacement can be devastating. Children are particularly vulnerable, facing significant risks of exploitation and abuse. Ultimately, the current state of the European asylum system falls short of the international legal obligations to provide protection to those seeking refuge. It creates further trauma, instability, and disillusionment for those individuals seeking protection in the EU. This situation demands an urgent and fundamental re-evaluation of the system, pushing for transformative change, not minor adjustments. The need for a just and effective asylum system necessitates a comprehensive approach that addresses the systemic issues, embraces human rights, and is underpinned by the spirit of international cooperation and mutual responsibility.

3 Asylum in North America

The United States and Canada, while geographically proximate, demonstrate distinct approaches to asylum processing. The US system, characterized by a complex multi-layered bureaucracy involving Customs and Border Protection (CBP), United States Citizenship and Immigration Services (USCIS), and the Executive Office for Immigration Review (EOIR), often leads to significant backlogs. This complexity, coupled with varying interpretations of legal precedent across different immigration courts, creates inconsistencies in adjudication. Applicants navigate a challenging landscape, where the burden of proof rests heavily on them to convincingly establish a well-founded fear of persecution. Successfully demonstrating past persecution, or a credible fear of future persecution based on race, religion, nationality, political opinion, or membership in a particular social group, demands meticulous documentation and compelling testimony. The sheer volume of cases, coupled with resource constraints, contributes to lengthy processing times, potentially leaving asylum seekers in a state of protracted uncertainty. Moreover, the Trump administration's restrictive policies, including the 'Remain in Mexico' protocol and limitations on asylum eligibility, significantly impacted access to protection and created a humanitarian crisis at the border, exacerbating existing challenges.

In contrast, Canada's asylum system operates with a more centralized structure. While still involving different agencies, the process often appears less fragmented than its southern neighbor's. Although facing its own backlogs, Canada generally provides more streamlined pathways for processing claims. While the burden of proof remains on the applicant, the Canadian system often appears more receptive to claims of well-founded fear. However, both countries grapple with issues of detention, access to legal representation, and adequate support for asylum seekers awaiting decisions, often compounded by bureaucratic inefficiency. The difference in approaches highlights the varied interpretations and implementations of international refugee law, even within a geographically similar context. Furthermore, both nations contend with the challenges of managing irregular migration, differentiating between genuine asylum seekers and those seeking economic opportunities, often blurring the lines and resulting in differing levels of scrutiny, resulting in inconsistencies in application and creating inequalities in access to protection.

Understanding these nuanced differences requires careful analysis of each nation's legal framework, its judicial interpretations, and the practical realities faced by asylum seekers navigating the system. The variations in processing times, access to legal aid, and the overall effectiveness of each system are critical considerations. Research into the impact of specific policies, like the aforementioned 'Remain in Mexico' policy, reveals the significant consequences on the lives of asylum seekers, highlighting the need for a more humane and efficient approach to handling asylum claims. The comparative study of the asylum procedures in the US and Canada offers valuable insights into the strengths and weaknesses of each system, providing a foundation for potential reforms. Furthermore, examining the socio-political context of each country, including public attitudes toward immigration and the level of governmental resources dedicated to asylum processing, offers a more complete understanding.

The disparity in outcomes between the two nations underscores the need for a more standardized, equitable, and efficient approach to asylum processing. This analysis should incorporate research on successful models of asylum processing, including those in other developed countries, as well as the examination of best practices identified by international organizations such as the UNHCR. The goal should be to develop systems that both effectively determine who qualifies for protection while ensuring that those needing refuge have access to a just and efficient process. Advocacy for improved access to legal representation, as well as increased resources for processing applications, remains crucial in ensuring a fair and effective asylum system that upholds the principles of international refugee law, providing a benchmark for future improvements to the systems in place. Equitable solutions require a multi-pronged approach involving legislative reforms, increased funding, and improved coordination between government agencies, combined with a focus on addressing the root causes of displacement and promoting international cooperation in addressing the global refugee crisis. Only then can both countries truly align their policies with the international legal frameworks established for the protection of asylum seekers.

3.1 US Asylum System

The United States asylum system, a complex and often criticized mechanism, operates under a framework established primarily by the Immigration and Nationality Act (INA). This legislation, while aiming to provide refuge for those fleeing persecution, has been subject to significant changes and interpretations over time, leading to inconsistent outcomes and persistent challenges. The process begins with an applicant filing a Form I-589, Application for Asylum and for Withholding of Removal, detailing their fear of persecution in their home country. This necessitates a clear and compelling narrative, often requiring legal assistance to navigate the intricacies of the law and effectively present a credible case. Subsequent steps involve various screenings and interviews with asylum officers, followed by a hearing before an immigration judge should the initial application be denied.

Successful asylum claims require demonstrating a well-founded fear of persecution based on race, religion, nationality, political opinion, or membership in a particular social group. This "well-founded fear" standard necessitates a convincing argument that demonstrates a substantial likelihood of persecution should the applicant be returned to their home country. The evidentiary burden rests heavily on the applicant, requiring them to provide substantial documentation and credible testimony to support their claim. The process can be arduous, often involving protracted delays and significant emotional and financial strain. Many applicants face difficulties securing legal representation, further compounding the challenges they encounter.

One notable aspect of the US asylum system is its reliance on immigration courts, separate from the regular federal court system. These courts, often overwhelmed by a substantial backlog of cases, have faced scrutiny regarding their efficiency and impartiality. The sheer volume of cases coupled with limited resources can lead to lengthy delays, forcing applicants to endure prolonged periods of uncertainty and vulnerability. Furthermore, criticism has been leveled at the consistency of judicial decisions, with variations in interpretations contributing to inconsistencies in outcomes. Decisions made at this stage are critical and can significantly impact an individual's future.

The role of credible fear interviews is also crucial. This initial assessment determines whether an applicant's fear of persecution is sufficient to warrant a full hearing. Negative outcomes at this stage can effectively end an asylum application before it has a chance to fully proceed through the legal processes, resulting in deportation or a return to an environment where persecution is likely. Therefore, this initial screening holds immense importance, particularly given that many applicants lack the legal assistance needed to effectively present their case during these crucial stages. The intricacies of immigration law, combined with language barriers and cultural differences, exacerbate these challenges.

Beyond the legal intricacies, the social and political climate significantly influences the US asylum system. Public opinion, political discourse, and administrative policies all play a role in shaping the overall efficacy and fairness of the system. Changes in administrations frequently lead to shifts in policies, impacting application processing times, acceptance rates, and overall access to asylum procedures. This susceptibility to political shifts creates inconsistencies and uncertainties for those seeking refuge within the US. Navigating these fluctuating elements adds another layer of complexity to an already challenging process. Ultimately, the US asylum system, while intended to provide protection, is a constantly evolving landscape, reflecting the interplay between legal frameworks, administrative processes, and political realities. Its effectiveness and fairness remain subjects of ongoing debate and reform efforts.

3.2 Canadian Asylum System

Canada's asylum system, unlike its American counterpart, operates under a distinct legal framework. The Immigration and Refugee Protection Act (IRPA) of 2002 forms the cornerstone of this system, establishing a comprehensive process for determining refugee claims. Central to this act is the principle of non-refoulement, a commitment to not returning individuals to places where they face a well-founded fear of persecution. This principle, enshrined in international law, guides the entire Canadian asylum procedure ensuring a level of protection.

Unlike some systems with multiple stages of appeal, Canada's system generally involves a single decision at the Immigration and Refugee Board (IRB). The IRB, an independent administrative tribunal, hears refugee claims and renders decisions based on the evidence presented. Applicants must demonstrate a well-founded fear of persecution based on specific grounds such as race, religion, nationality, political opinion, or membership in a particular social group. This requires compelling evidence, often including documentation, witness testimony, and country information reports outlining the risks faced in the applicant's home country. The evidentiary standard is a key differentiator between jurisdictions and Canada has consistently faced scrutiny about its efficacy.

The process begins with an applicant submitting a claim, which triggers an initial assessment by Immigration, Refugees and Citizenship Canada (IRCC). This initial screening determines admissibility and flags potentially unfounded claims, a crucial step in managing the high volume of applications, ensuring that resources are used efficiently. Those deemed admissible proceed to the IRB for a hearing, where they present their case before a member of the Board, with the assistance of legal counsel if they choose. They meticulously present their personal narrative, providing comprehensive details about their background, reasons for fleeing their homeland, and fears of return. The IRB member then assesses the credibility of their account and weighs it against available evidence and country information, a careful balancing act that requires in-depth analysis.

Decisions of the IRB can be appealed to the Federal Court, providing a crucial avenue for judicial review. This appeals process ensures that the decisions are consistent with the law and are procedurally fair. It allows for a second examination of the evidence, affording protection from potential mistakes or biases during the initial assessment. However, access to legal counsel is not guaranteed which can pose a significant barrier, impacting the fairness of the proceedings for those with limited financial resources, making them more susceptible to an unfavorable outcome.

The Canadian system, despite its strengths, is not without its challenges. Backlogs at the IRB are a persistent concern. Delays in processing applications can lead to prolonged uncertainty and hardship for asylum seekers. Furthermore, the system's complexity can be daunting for those navigating it without legal representation. The requirement for comprehensive evidence, while essential for fairness, often presents difficulties for applicants lacking documentation or access to support networks. These difficulties, if not adequately addressed, can lead to an increase in successful appeals, highlighting the tension between the efficient administration of the system and ensuring fairness. The Canadian government's ongoing efforts to streamline the process and provide better support are crucial to addressing these issues.

Access to legal aid is a key determinant of successful outcomes. However, limited funding and long waitlists create substantial barriers. This disparity in access to legal counsel disproportionately affects vulnerable asylum seekers, who may be unaware of their rights or lack the resources to secure adequate representation, leaving them more vulnerable to deportation. This creates an inherent inequality within the system that needs to be resolved. Addressing this through increased funding for legal aid programs and providing clear, accessible information about legal rights would substantially improve the fairness and effectiveness of the process, reducing inconsistencies and unwarranted delays.

In recent years, Canada has seen increased numbers of asylum claims. This surge, coupled with existing challenges, highlights the need for ongoing review and reform. The government regularly updates its policies and procedures to reflect changing circumstances and international best practices, working continuously to improve processes. This ongoing evaluation is critical for maintaining a just and efficient system that balances the needs of asylum seekers with the capacity of the system. The commitment to continual improvement is essential for Canada's reputation as a just and equitable nation offering safe harbor to those fleeing persecution. Careful consideration of the broader socio-political context is needed to balance efficiency with compassionate and just treatment of asylum seekers, protecting their rights while maintaining a workable and efficient system.

4 Asylum Procedures in Australia

Australia's asylum procedures are complex and have undergone significant changes, often marked by controversy. The nation's approach, particularly its offshore processing policy, has drawn intense international scrutiny and legal challenges. This policy involves transferring asylum seekers arriving by boat to processing centers in countries like Nauru and Papua New Guinea, a practice criticized by human rights organizations for its potential to violate international law principles of non-refoulement and for the conditions within these centers. These criticisms have been consistently leveled against the government, highlighting concerns over the welfare of asylum seekers subjected to prolonged detention and often inadequate healthcare and mental health support. The legality of offshore processing has been repeatedly contested in Australian courts, with varying judgments reflecting the intricate legal and ethical dimensions of the issue.

Domestically, asylum seekers undergo a rigorous process involving initial assessments, interviews, and potential appeals. Applicants must demonstrate they meet the definition of a refugee under the Refugee Convention, proving a well-founded fear of persecution based on race, religion, nationality, political opinion, or membership of a particular social group. The burden of proof rests heavily on the asylum seeker, often requiring substantial evidence to support their claims. This process is lengthy and can be incredibly stressful for individuals already traumatized by their experiences. Many face bureaucratic hurdles and linguistic barriers, which can make the process more difficult to navigate. Furthermore, access to legal representation is crucial for a fair hearing but isn't always guaranteed, particularly for those who are unable to afford it.

Human rights concerns are central to the debate surrounding Australia's asylum policies. Reports from organizations like Human Rights Watch and Amnesty International have consistently documented allegations of human rights abuses within offshore processing centers, including instances of sexual assault, self-harm, and inadequate medical care. These reports detail the impact of prolonged detention on mental health, emphasizing the detrimental effects on vulnerable individuals, including children. The prolonged uncertainty surrounding their future exacerbates these mental health challenges and further underlines the considerable human cost of Australia's approach. International pressure to adopt more humane practices and uphold international human rights standards continues to mount.

Legal challenges to Australia's asylum policies have been ongoing and multifaceted. Litigation has focused on the legality of offshore processing, detention conditions, and the adequacy of procedural fairness in asylum claims. Significant court cases have addressed issues such as the right to seek asylum and the compatibility of Australian policies with international human rights law. The outcomes of these cases have had a variable impact on policy, with some judgments leading to minor reforms while others have been largely disregarded by the government, highlighting the tension between judicial review and executive power in the context of immigration policy.

Recent reforms to Australia's asylum framework have aimed to streamline processing, improve the efficiency of the system, and address some of the concerns raised by human rights organizations. However, these reforms have been met with mixed reactions. While the government often presents these as improvements to efficiency and effectiveness, critics argue they often do little to mitigate the fundamental human rights issues associated with offshore processing and prolonged detention. The ongoing debate reflects the persistent tension between the government's border security concerns and the humanitarian obligations associated with the protection of refugees. Ultimately, Australia's asylum procedures remain an area of ongoing debate, balancing security concerns with the protection of human rights and the legal obligations outlined in international law.

4.1 Offshore Processing

Australia's offshore processing of asylum seekers, primarily implemented on Nauru and Manus Island, has become a highly contentious issue, attracting significant international criticism. This policy, designed to deter asylum seekers from arriving by boat, involves transferring individuals seeking protection to processing centers located outside Australia's mainland. The legality and humanitarian implications of this approach have been consistently challenged, sparking intense debate among legal experts, human rights organizations, and the Australian public. The policy's core rationale is rooted in the belief that offshore processing will discourage irregular maritime arrivals, a belief constantly debated given the ongoing arrival of asylum seekers by other means.
The practicalities of offshore processing are complex. Asylum seekers undergo initial screenings in these off-shore centers, often facing lengthy delays and inadequate living conditions. Access to legal representation and fair procedures can be severely limited, raising serious concerns about the due process rights of those seeking protection. These individuals remain in a state of uncertainty for extended periods, impacting their mental and physical well-being. Reports regularly document inadequate healthcare, instances of self-harm, and the psychological trauma endured by individuals within the centers. The cost to Australia and the resulting humanitarian crisis challenge the very idea of effective and humane refugee processing.

Furthermore, the legality of offshore processing under international law is profoundly questionable. The principle of non-refoulement, a cornerstone of international refugee law, prohibits the return of a refugee to a place where they face a well-founded fear of persecution. Critics argue that offshore processing, in effect, circumvents this crucial protection by leaving asylum seekers in locations where their safety and well-being cannot be guaranteed. The argument that these offshore facilities aren't technically Australian soil has been frequently challenged in court and international forums, leading to an ongoing legal battle over the legality and morality of the policy.

The human cost associated with Australia's offshore processing policy is immense. The prolonged uncertainty, coupled with often deplorable living conditions and restricted access to essential services, severely impacts the mental and physical health of asylum seekers. Numerous reports from human rights organizations detail instances of abuse, neglect, and self-harm within the detention centers. Children, particularly vulnerable, are particularly impacted. Studies demonstrate a range of severe physical and psychological effects on the mental health of children and adults subjected to such indefinite detention, resulting in increased rates of mental illness, self-harm, and suicide attempts within the facilities. This humanitarian crisis has led to widespread condemnation from international bodies and human rights organizations.

The Australian government defends its policy by emphasizing its effectiveness in reducing irregular maritime arrivals. However, this claim is subject to ongoing debate, with studies suggesting alternative strategies may achieve similar results with considerably less detrimental impact on human rights. Critics point to the substantial cost of offshore processing, questioning whether these expenditures align with the long-term needs of genuine refugees. Indeed, evidence shows that many refugees and asylum seekers end up arriving to Australia via other routes, often paying significantly more to human smugglers and facing even greater dangers along the way, negating the deterrence effect and proving the policy's cost-ineffectiveness. The complex and ongoing legal challenges to the policy highlight the inherent tension between national security concerns and the fundamental human rights of vulnerable individuals seeking protection. A thorough evaluation of alternative, more humane and cost-effective approaches is essential to address this complex and enduring crisis. The ongoing debate emphasizes the need for a comprehensive reassessment of Australia's refugee policy, incorporating international legal standards and a commitment to safeguarding human rights.

4.2 Domestic Procedures

Australia's domestic asylum procedures are complex and frequently contested. Applicants initiate the process by lodging a protection visa application with the Department of Home Affairs. This application requires detailed documentation substantiating their claim, including evidence of persecution or well-founded fear of persecution based on race, religion, nationality, political opinion, or membership of a particular social group. The process can be lengthy and arduous, demanding significant time, resources and resilience from the applicant. This initial stage includes thorough background checks and security assessments, sometimes involving multiple interviews. The sheer volume of applications received by the Department often leads to significant processing delays, leaving applicants in a state of prolonged uncertainty. Support services, while available, frequently fall short of meeting the complex and evolving needs of a vulnerable population.

The assessment of protection visa applications often involves a two-step process. Firstly, a departmental officer assesses the application based on the submitted evidence. This initial assessment may involve further inquiries. If the officer deems the claim is not credible, the application is refused. Conversely, if the officer finds the claim credible, it proceeds to a second stage. This second stage usually involves a hearing before the Refugee Review Tribunal, an independent statutory body responsible for determining whether an applicant meets the criteria for refugee status under the Refugee Convention. Tribunal hearings, while providing a crucial procedural safeguard, can be intimidating for asylum seekers unfamiliar with legal processes and the Australian judicial system. This often necessitates the engagement of legal representation, adding another layer of complexity to an already challenging situation. Moreover, legal aid services are often insufficient to meet the overwhelming demand. This disproportionately affects vulnerable applicants who lack the financial resources to secure effective legal representation.

Decisions made by the Refugee Review Tribunal are appealable to the Federal Circuit Court and, subsequently, the Federal Court. These avenues provide further procedural safeguards for applicants who disagree with the Tribunal's assessment. However, the costs associated with legal representation at this stage are even higher. Moreover, the appellate process can be protracted, adding even more time to an already lengthy asylum application. The resulting uncertainty can have significant psychological and social impacts, potentially exacerbating existing trauma and creating additional hardship for asylum seekers. The lack of timely legal aid can often mean the best outcome for the applicant may not be achieved. This aspect underlines the crucial role of accessible and efficient legal aid in ensuring fairness and justice within Australia's asylum system.

The Australian government has implemented various policies aimed at streamlining the asylum process and deterring unauthorised arrivals. These policies, while purportedly designed to enhance efficiency, have raised considerable concerns about their impact on human rights and due process. The use of offshore processing, for example, has been widely criticised for its potential to violate the principle of non-refoulement. Critics highlight the lack of access to appropriate legal representation and fair hearing procedures in offshore detention centers. These concerns extend to the conditions within these centres, often reported as substandard and detrimental to the physical and psychological wellbeing of asylum seekers. The long-term consequences of these policies on the mental health of refugees are concerning, often leading to increased rates of anxiety, depression, and post-traumatic stress disorder. Consequently, a broader, more humanitarian approach is needed to address these issues.

In conclusion, Australia's domestic asylum procedures are characterised by significant complexities, inefficiencies, and challenges related to human rights. Whilst the system provides a framework for determining refugee status and ensuring procedural fairness, the high volume of applications, extensive processing times, and limitations in access to legal aid often result in undue delays and hardships for asylum seekers. Furthermore, the controversial policies implemented to deter irregular migration have raised serious human rights concerns. Reform efforts should prioritize improvements to the efficiency and accessibility of the system whilst upholding the principles of non-refoulement and ensuring procedural fairness for all asylum seekers. A more streamlined and efficient system coupled with comprehensive access to legal representation and adequate support services could significantly enhance the human rights protections afforded to asylum seekers within the Australian system. The government needs to acknowledge that the ultimate goal should be to balance the need for efficient border security with the protection of the rights of vulnerable individuals seeking asylum.

4.3 Human Rights Concerns

Australia's offshore processing of asylum seekers, particularly on Nauru and Manus Island, has drawn considerable international condemnation. The conditions in these facilities have been widely documented as substandard, with reports of inadequate healthcare, psychological trauma, and violence. These practices raise serious questions about Australia's commitment to its human rights obligations under international law, specifically the principle of non-refoulement. The prolonged detention of asylum seekers, often for years, without access to adequate legal representation or fair and efficient processing, also constitutes a breach of fundamental human rights.

The indefinite detention of children, especially in such harsh conditions, is particularly egregious. International human rights law explicitly prohibits the arbitrary detention of children, emphasizing the need for their best interests to be the primary consideration in all decisions affecting them. The Australian government's policies have been criticized for failing to comply with this fundamental principle, leading to significant and lasting psychological harm to vulnerable children. The long-term impact on their development and well-being is a considerable concern for human rights organizations and international bodies.

Legal challenges to Australia's offshore processing policy have been ongoing. Numerous court cases have highlighted the illegality of indefinite detention and the inadequacy of the process, yet the government has persisted with these policies, often relying on national security concerns or border protection arguments to justify the infringement of fundamental human rights. These justifications have been increasingly scrutinized by human rights activists and legal experts, who argue that national security considerations cannot override the state's obligations to protect human rights. The interplay between national security imperatives and human rights protection remains a complex and contentious issue in Australia's refugee policy debate.

The impact on asylum seekers' mental health is profound and well-documented. Prolonged detention, coupled with the uncertainty surrounding their future and the harsh conditions in detention centers, contributes to high rates of anxiety, depression, self-harm, and post-traumatic stress disorder. The lack of adequate mental health care within the detention facilities exacerbates these problems, leaving many asylum seekers with severe and long-lasting mental health issues. These are not merely statistics; they are individual human tragedies, underscoring the ethical and human rights failings of the current system.

Beyond the physical and mental health consequences, the offshore processing policy has profound implications for access to justice. Asylum seekers are often held in remote locations, far from legal representation and support networks, making it extremely difficult to access fair and efficient legal processes. This effectively denies them access to fundamental legal safeguards and contributes to the perpetuation of human rights violations. The geographical isolation contributes to a sense of powerlessness and despair, further undermining their well-being. This lack of access to justice is a systemic issue that fundamentally undermines the fairness of the asylum process.

Furthermore, the Australian government's policies have been criticized for fostering a climate of xenophobia and discrimination. The rhetoric surrounding border protection and national security often fuels negative public perceptions of asylum seekers, leading to prejudice and social exclusion. This contributes to a hostile environment where asylum seekers are less likely to find support and integration opportunities. This societal impact must be considered as a crucial component of the human rights analysis of Australia's asylum policies.

The human rights concerns surrounding Australia's asylum policies demand urgent attention. Reforms must prioritize the protection of fundamental human rights, upholding the principles of non-refoulement, due process, and the best interests of the child. A shift towards community-based alternatives to detention, along with improvements to the asylum processing system, is essential to ensure that Australia's obligations under international human rights law are met. This requires a fundamental reassessment of the government's approach and a concerted effort to create a more humane and just system for asylum seekers. The international community's scrutiny of these practices is crucial in holding Australia accountable to its human rights responsibilities. Only through a commitment to human dignity and respect for the rule of law can Australia address the profound human rights challenges posed by its asylum system.

4.4 Legal Challenges

Navigating Australia's asylum system presents numerous legal hurdles. The government's offshore processing policy, for instance, has faced consistent legal challenges, often centering on the legality of indefinite detention and the potential violation of international human rights law, particularly the principle of non-refoulement. These challenges frequently involve arguments that offshore processing infringes on the right to seek asylum, the right to a fair hearing, and the right to be free from torture and cruel, inhuman, or degrading treatment. The High Court of Australia has been frequently involved in deciding these cases, and their decisions often shape the legal landscape for refugee protection within Australia.

Many legal challenges arise from the interpretation and application of Australia's Migration Act. This legislation, while designed to manage migration flows, often comes under scrutiny for its perceived harshness and incompatibility with international human rights standards. For example, the Act's provisions on visa cancellations and mandatory detention have been the subject of numerous court cases, leading to judicial reviews and appeals. These cases often highlight the disparity between legal provisions and the practical realities faced by asylum seekers.

The legal battles often focus on procedural fairness. Asylum seekers must meet stringent evidentiary standards to prove their claims, requiring them to present substantial evidence to substantiate their fear of persecution. This burden of proof can be challenging to meet, especially considering the often-traumatic experiences that asylum seekers have endured. The legal challenges in these instances frequently question the fairness of the process, highlighting the difficulties faced in meeting the required evidence standards while dealing with the psychological impacts of past trauma and the lack of documentation.

Another significant area of legal contention revolves around the definition of "refugee" under Australian law and its alignment with international conventions. Cases often arise where the interpretation of the Refugee Convention and its application within the Australian legal framework are contested. The inconsistencies between international law and domestic legislation have frequently resulted in protracted legal battles, with the outcome of these cases often influencing the eligibility criteria for asylum seekers and the overall effectiveness of Australia's refugee protection system.

Furthermore, the intersection between national security concerns and the rights of asylum seekers poses significant legal difficulties. The government's efforts to balance national security with human rights have been a constant source of contention, leading to numerous legal challenges that examine the proportionality of measures taken to safeguard national security and their impact on the rights of asylum seekers. This area of law requires careful balancing of competing national interests and international human rights obligations.

The effectiveness of legal aid and access to justice for asylum seekers represents a crucial aspect of the legal landscape. The availability of legal representation and resources varies considerably, potentially exacerbating the challenges faced by asylum seekers who may find themselves navigating a complex legal system with limited assistance. This disparity in access to justice underscores the importance of ensuring equitable access to legal services for all asylum seekers, regardless of their circumstances. The long-term implication of this unequal access to justice affects the fundamental rights of this vulnerable population.

Finally, the ongoing evolution of Australia's asylum policies and legislation introduces another layer of legal complexities. Amendments to the Migration Act and shifts in government policy often trigger fresh rounds of legal challenges, creating a dynamic and ever-changing legal environment that requires ongoing analysis and adaptation from both legal professionals and asylum seekers alike. Understanding these shifts and their implications is crucial for anyone involved in this complex field. The constant state of flux demands continuous attention and adaptation to keep pace with the evolving legal standards and precedents.

4.5 Recent Reforms

Australia's asylum policies have undergone significant changes in recent years, marked by a shift towards a more restrictive approach. The emphasis has moved from onshore processing to offshore processing, a controversial measure that involves transferring asylum seekers to facilities in countries like Nauru and Papua New Guinea. This strategy, justified by the government as a deterrent to irregular migration, has faced considerable criticism from human rights organizations and international bodies. Concerns have been raised about the conditions in offshore detention centers, allegations of human rights abuses, and the mental health impact on detainees.

The legal battles surrounding these policies are extensive. Numerous court cases have challenged the legality of offshore processing, raising questions about Australia's compliance with international refugee law, particularly the principle of non-refoulement. While the government has consistently defended its policies, the legal challenges have highlighted the complexities and potential inconsistencies between national policy and international legal obligations. The High Court of Australia has played a crucial role in these legal battles, shaping the legal landscape of asylum procedures and influencing the government's policy adjustments.

One notable recent reform involves the introduction of stricter visa requirements and increased scrutiny of asylum claims. The government has implemented more stringent evidentiary standards, requiring asylum seekers to provide more compelling evidence to support their claims. This shift towards a more restrictive approach has intensified concerns regarding the fairness and efficiency of the asylum process. Critics argue that these stricter requirements disproportionately affect vulnerable asylum seekers who may lack access to legal representation or sufficient documentation to substantiate their claims, ultimately hindering their access to protection.

Further reforms concentrate on streamlining the processing of asylum claims, aimed at reducing backlogs and improving efficiency. While the intention is laudable, critics express concern that prioritization of speed over due process could compromise the quality of decision-making and jeopardize fair consideration of individual cases. Concerns remain about the potential for errors and injustices within a system prioritizing speed over thorough investigation. Such a system increases the chances of errors and the potential for arbitrary and unfair decisions.

Another significant area of reform focuses on the integration of asylum seekers into Australian society. Programs aimed at assisting successful asylum seekers with employment, housing, and language acquisition have been implemented. This recognizes the importance of providing a pathway for integration and contributing to a more inclusive society. However, critics argue these initiatives are insufficient to address the systemic disadvantages faced by many refugees in accessing essential services and achieving social and economic self-sufficiency. These reforms lack the necessary scope to address the deep-seated systemic challenges faced by many refugees in accessing essential services and achieving social and economic self-sufficiency.

In conclusion, Australia's recent reforms reflect a complex interplay of security concerns, domestic political pressures, and international legal obligations. While the government emphasizes its commitment to a robust and efficient asylum system, critics contend that several reforms have compromised the principles of fairness, due process, and human rights protection, particularly concerning offshore processing and the stricter evidentiary standards imposed on asylum seekers. The long-term implications of these reforms for Australia's international reputation and its commitment to international refugee law remain a subject of ongoing debate and legal scrutiny. Further research and analysis are needed to assess the effectiveness and human rights impact of these sweeping changes to the country's asylum processes. Ultimately, the ongoing tension between national security priorities and international human rights obligations remains a defining characteristic of Australia's approach to refugee protection. The effectiveness and fairness of these recent reforms, therefore, will continue to be a subject of critical evaluation and ongoing debate amongst policymakers, human rights advocates, and legal scholars alike, highlighting the enduring challenges inherent in balancing national interests with international legal obligations in the complex realm of refugee protection.

5 Asylum in Africa

The African continent, a vast and diverse landscape, presents a complex tapestry of asylum practices. Unlike the more unified systems seen in Europe or North America, African nations grapple with a unique set of challenges, heavily influenced by persistent conflict, widespread poverty, and varying levels of state capacity. Regional frameworks, such as the Organization of African Unity (OAU) Convention Governing the Specific Aspects of Refugee Problems in Africa, offer a foundational legal structure, yet their implementation remains uneven across the continent. The OAU Convention, while significant, lacks the comprehensive reach and robust enforcement mechanisms seen in the 1951 Refugee Convention. This disparity underscores the deeply contextual nature of asylum in Africa.

Many African nations struggle with significant internal displacement, alongside large numbers of refugees from neighboring countries. This frequently strains already limited resources, leading to inconsistent application of asylum procedures and frequently inadequate provision of basic necessities for those seeking refuge. The sheer scale of humanitarian crises often overwhelms national capacities, resulting in protracted periods of uncertainty and vulnerability for asylum seekers. This contrasts sharply with the (relatively) well-resourced systems found in certain developed nations. Furthermore, weak governance structures and corruption can further impede the effective protection of refugees, leading to exploitation and human rights violations.

National practices vary enormously. Some countries boast relatively progressive legal frameworks, actively engaging with international standards and providing reasonable levels of support to asylum seekers. Others, hampered by internal conflict or political instability, offer little in the way of formal protection. In these situations, refugees often find themselves reliant on the goodwill of local communities or humanitarian organizations, a precarious existence subject to the whims of circumstance. This inherent instability is a stark contrast to the more formalized and (ideally) predictable processes of Western asylum systems. The lack of standardized procedures and consistent enforcement creates a significant vulnerability for those seeking safety within the African context.

Consider, for instance, the experiences of refugees fleeing conflict in the Sahel region. Many find themselves traversing dangerous and unpredictable routes, often at the mercy of human traffickers and exposed to various forms of violence and exploitation. Reaching a place of safety is only the first hurdle; securing asylum and integrating into a new community often proves equally, if not more, challenging. Accessing basic services like healthcare, education, and employment becomes a constant struggle, as overwhelmed governments and under-resourced NGOs fight to keep up with the demands. Such realities highlight the deep-seated discrepancies between the ideal of international refugee law and the often harsh realities on the ground.

The legal frameworks themselves often reflect the challenges. Many African countries have adopted national legislation that addresses refugee protection, but these laws vary widely in scope and effectiveness. Some closely align with international standards, while others contain significant limitations or ambiguities, leading to inconsistent application and interpretation. Furthermore, the enforcement capacity of these laws is often weak, hindering their practical effect on the ground. This lack of consistent application often leaves asylum seekers vulnerable to arbitrary detention, deportation, or other human rights abuses.

Therefore, achieving effective refugee protection in Africa requires a multi-faceted approach. Strengthening national legal frameworks and building the capacity of government institutions are crucial steps. This includes providing training for immigration officials, judges, and other relevant personnel on international refugee law and human rights standards. Equally important is the need to foster greater regional cooperation and coordination to share best practices and address common challenges. This collaborative approach could involve joint training programs, information-sharing mechanisms, and standardized asylum procedures across borders.
International organizations and donor countries have a vital role to play in supporting these efforts. Providing technical assistance, financial resources, and capacity-building programs can help African nations strengthen their asylum systems and better protect refugees. However, this support must be aligned with national priorities and capacities, ensuring that interventions are sustainable and locally relevant. The path forward necessitates a delicate balance between upholding international standards and responding to the unique circumstances and limitations of each nation. Ultimately, the aim is to move towards a more equitable and effective system that provides meaningful protection for refugees throughout the African continent, acknowledging the unique context and the vital necessity of tailored solutions. The journey towards a comprehensive and humane approach will undoubtedly require sustained commitment and collaborative action on multiple levels.

5.1 Regional Frameworks

The African landscape presents a complex tapestry of legal and political realities when it comes to refugee protection. Unlike Europe's relatively unified, albeit often strained, system, Africa's approach is significantly more fragmented, shaped by diverse historical contexts, varying levels of state capacity, and the constant pressure of ongoing conflicts and displacement. The Organization of African Unity (OAU) Convention governing the specific aspects of refugees, while laudable in its intentions, often faces challenges in its practical implementation. Many states, grappling with their own internal struggles and limited resources, struggle to meet the convention's stipulations effectively. This creates inconsistencies in application and protection levels across the continent. Furthermore, the sheer volume of internally displaced persons (IDPs) and cross-border refugees often overwhelms the existing infrastructure and capacity of many nations.

Consequently, refugee protection in Africa isn't uniformly applied. Certain countries, boasting more stable governance and resources, may offer relatively robust systems. Others, burdened by conflict or poverty, may offer little more than basic survival support, often leaving refugees vulnerable to exploitation and abuse. The lack of consistent legal frameworks across the continent contributes to this disparity. Legal definitions of a "refugee" can fluctuate, resulting in inconsistent eligibility criteria for protection. Enforcement mechanisms are often weak, leading to a lack of accountability for violations of refugee rights. There is a significant need for strengthening national legal frameworks. This includes clarifying definitions, establishing clear procedures, and improving access to justice for asylum seekers.

The inconsistent application of international legal norms across various African nations highlights another critical aspect. While the OAU Convention provides a foundational framework, its implementation and interpretation vary considerably. National laws often either fall short of the Convention's standards or incorporate provisions that conflict with international law. This disparity creates significant challenges for refugees, particularly those attempting to navigate the process across national borders. The lack of harmonization across national laws contributes to legal uncertainty and administrative inconsistencies, making it difficult for refugees to secure adequate protection. Regional cooperation is essential to address this issue. Sharing best practices, harmonizing legal frameworks, and establishing joint mechanisms for processing asylum claims can help create a more equitable and consistent system across the continent.

Moreover, the effectiveness of existing regional frameworks is hindered by a range of factors. Political instability and ongoing conflicts in many parts of Africa severely impact the ability of states to provide adequate protection. Weak state capacity, characterized by limited resources, inadequate infrastructure, and a shortage of trained personnel, further compounds the problem. Corruption can also significantly undermine the integrity of the asylum system, leaving refugees vulnerable to bribery and extortion. Strengthening state capacity through international aid, targeted training programs, and technical assistance is vital for improving refugee protection. These efforts should prioritize capacity building in areas such as legal frameworks, border management, refugee registration, and humanitarian assistance.

Furthermore, external factors significantly influence the asylum landscape in Africa. The displacement crises in neighboring countries often place additional pressure on already strained resources. This influx of refugees can exacerbate existing social and economic tensions, making it more challenging for host countries to provide adequate protection. The international community plays a crucial role in supporting African states in their efforts to protect refugees. This includes providing financial assistance, technical support, and sharing expertise on best practices. Promoting regional cooperation and fostering a spirit of solidarity among African nations is also crucial in addressing the challenges associated with refugee flows. This involves collaborative efforts in addressing the root causes of displacement, fostering economic development, and strengthening regional mechanisms for refugee protection. Ultimately, comprehensive and sustainable solutions require a holistic approach that tackles the underlying political, economic, and social factors that contribute to displacement and refugee flows across the continent. Long-term solutions need coordinated strategies to address the root causes of displacement, promote sustainable development, and ensure that states possess both the capacity and the will to effectively uphold the rights of refugees.

5.2 National Practices

Numerous African nations grapple with significant refugee influxes, often stemming from protracted conflicts and widespread instability. These circumstances frequently overwhelm already strained resources and infrastructure, leading to inconsistent application of international refugee law. While many states have ratified the 1951 Refugee Convention and its 1967 Protocol, the translation of these legal obligations into effective national policies remains uneven. This disparity is often fueled by a lack of capacity, limited financial resources, and the absence of robust legal frameworks specifically designed to manage refugee claims efficiently and humanely. Furthermore, political will sometimes proves insufficient to prioritize refugee protection above other pressing national concerns.

The diversity of national practices is striking. Some nations operate relatively efficient asylum systems, relying on a streamlined process and offering adequate support to asylum seekers. Others struggle to establish even rudimentary procedures, leading to lengthy processing times, bureaucratic hurdles, and a lack of appropriate reception conditions. Access to legal aid remains a critical challenge throughout much of the continent. The availability of legal representation significantly impacts an asylum seeker's chances of a successful claim, yet many find themselves navigating a complex system without adequate support, often falling victim to systemic inequalities. These disparities highlight the urgent need for improved access to justice and the strengthening of legal aid services for vulnerable individuals fleeing persecution.

Consider the significant variations in how countries define "refugee" status. While the international definition provides a framework, national interpretations can differ considerably, particularly regarding the assessment of well-founded fears of persecution. Some countries may adopt a narrower interpretation, resulting in a higher rejection rate for asylum claims. Others may demonstrate more leniency in their assessments, yet still struggle to provide adequate resources and support to those granted refugee status. A lack of clarity and consistency in defining key legal terms contributes to ambiguity and challenges in implementing the principles of non-refoulement. This variability necessitates a deeper examination of these diverse approaches to better comprehend the factors influencing national-level interpretations and how they affect those seeking refuge.

Furthermore, the capacity of national immigration and refugee agencies significantly influences how effectively states implement international standards. Under-resourced agencies with limited staff and inadequate training can lead to delays in processing claims, potentially exposing vulnerable individuals to prolonged uncertainty and hardship. Effective refugee protection requires not only legal frameworks, but also practical mechanisms for their implementation. Capacity building initiatives focusing on training, resource allocation, and improved data management are essential to improving the efficacy of national systems. It is equally crucial to address systemic corruption and promote transparency to guarantee fair and impartial processes. Addressing these systematic shortcomings is crucial to ensuring that national procedures align with international legal obligations.

The socio-political context often dramatically influences national practices. Countries experiencing internal conflict or instability frequently face immense challenges in protecting refugees. Political agendas and national security concerns can sometimes override humanitarian obligations. This necessitates exploring the political dynamics influencing asylum decision-making and understanding how broader societal attitudes towards refugees impact policy development and implementation. It's vital to acknowledge that the challenges facing African nations are multifaceted, highlighting the interconnectedness of political stability, economic conditions, and the capacity to effectively manage refugee flows. A comprehensive approach, engaging not only governmental bodies but also civil society organizations, is necessary to foster sustainable solutions that uphold both the rule of law and refugee rights. The complexity of the issues underscores the need for international cooperation and support to assist these nations in fulfilling their international obligations.

6 Comparative Analysis of Legal Frameworks

The preceding chapters have illuminated the diverse and often disparate approaches to asylum procedures globally. This chapter aims to synthesize those observations, offering a comparative analysis that highlights both best practices and significant deficiencies within these frameworks. By examining strengths and weaknesses across various jurisdictions—from the relatively well-established systems of North America to the more nascent and often strained systems in Africa—we can identify common threads and areas ripe for improvement. A crucial aspect involves understanding the inherent tensions between national security concerns and the fundamental human rights of asylum seekers. Many nations grapple with balancing these competing interests, leading to policies that are, at times, contradictory and ultimately ineffective.

Consider the contrasting approaches to offshore processing. Australia's controversial policy, while aiming to deter irregular migration, has drawn widespread condemnation for its human rights implications, documented by numerous human rights organizations and international bodies. This stands in stark contrast to the generally more integrated approaches adopted in Canada and parts of Europe, where processing occurs primarily within national borders. This difference underscores the significant ethical and practical ramifications of differing policy choices. The effectiveness of each approach in achieving its stated goals remains a complex and debated topic.

One notable strength observed in several jurisdictions is the increasing emphasis on legal representation for asylum seekers. Access to legal counsel is undeniably crucial for a fair and effective asylum process, ensuring that individuals understand their rights and can effectively present their cases. However, even where legal aid is provided, disparities persist in the quality and availability of such services, highlighting a persistent need for systemic improvements. Furthermore, the differing standards of proof required across jurisdictions introduce an element of inequity, impacting the success rates of asylum claims and raising concerns about the consistency of protection offered.

The speed and efficiency of processing also vary significantly. Some nations boast relatively swift processing times, while others face massive backlogs, leaving asylum seekers in protracted uncertainty and precarious conditions. This delay not only inflicts emotional distress but also affects the ability of individuals to integrate successfully into their host societies. Efficient and fair processing is a cornerstone of a robust asylum system, ensuring that genuine refugees receive timely protection, while also allowing for the swift processing of unfounded claims.

Furthermore, the treatment of asylum seekers during the processing period varies greatly across countries. Reception conditions range from reasonably adequate to inhumane, impacting significantly the well-being of those seeking refuge. Conditions of detention, when employed, can be particularly problematic, and the lack of access to essential services, such as healthcare and education, frequently compounds the vulnerability of asylum seekers. This inconsistency in the treatment of asylum seekers during the asylum-seeking process further underscores the need for increased cooperation and alignment of standards on a global scale.

Moving forward, we must acknowledge the inextricable link between effective asylum systems and robust international cooperation. The sharing of best practices, strengthened coordination mechanisms, and the establishment of

clear, consistent standards are paramount. This includes addressing the root causes of displacement, such as conflict and persecution, through diplomatic efforts and targeted aid. A truly effective international approach requires collaborative efforts, mutual respect for national sovereignty and a shared commitment to uphold fundamental human rights for all.
Ultimately, a fair and effective asylum system requires a multi-faceted approach, encompassing a commitment to due process, efficient processing, humane reception conditions, and robust legal representation. While many jurisdictions demonstrate elements of best practice, significant challenges remain in ensuring consistent and equitable treatment of asylum seekers worldwide. The ongoing need for reform and strengthened international cooperation is not merely a matter of humanitarian concern; it is essential for the maintenance of international stability and the upholding of universal human rights. Only through a concerted and collaborative global effort can we strive toward a world where all individuals seeking protection are treated with dignity and fairness. The task is undeniably challenging, yet the moral imperative remains compelling.

6.1 Strengths and Weaknesses

Many asylum systems globally share common strengths, yet significant weaknesses persist. The strength of international legal frameworks, primarily the 1951 Refugee Convention and its 1967 Protocol, provides a foundational standard for refugee protection, enshrining the principle of non-refoulement – the prohibition of returning refugees to places where they face danger. This principle, while not universally implemented effectively, forms a crucial ethical and legal cornerstone, influencing national legislation and judicial decisions in numerous countries. However, the application of this convention varies greatly across nations, resulting in inconsistencies in the protection afforded to refugees. The broad definition of a "refugee" within the convention can create challenges in practical application, particularly when dealing with situations of mixed migration flows, including economic migrants.

Despite the variations in national application, the existence of formal asylum procedures in most countries represents a significant strength. These processes, even when flawed, provide a mechanism for individuals to claim protection and have their claims assessed, offering a route to safety and legal status. While the procedures themselves differ dramatically – varying in speed, fairness, and transparency – the mere presence of a formal process distinguishes states committed to international standards from those that routinely violate them. Yet, many of these processes are backlogged, under-resourced, or subject to political interference, significantly diminishing their effectiveness. This creates situations where legitimate asylum seekers are left in prolonged legal limbo, facing precarious living conditions and uncertainties about their future.

The strength of some systems lies in their robust judicial review mechanisms. Countries with strong, independent judiciaries allow for appeals against negative asylum decisions, offering a critical check on administrative errors or biases. This provides a crucial safeguard against wrongful deportations and ensures accountability within the system. However, even in states with robust judicial review, access to legal representation can be a significant obstacle for asylum seekers, particularly those lacking financial resources. Without legal aid, many find themselves unable to navigate complex legal processes effectively, even if avenues for appeal exist. The disparity in access to justice creates an uneven playing field, undermining the fairness and impartiality of the system.

Another weakness commonly observed lies in the conditions faced by asylum seekers while their claims are processed. Many countries house asylum seekers in detention centers, raising significant human rights concerns, particularly regarding the length of detention and living conditions. These conditions can cause significant psychological trauma and undermine the dignity of those seeking refuge. Moreover, detention often exacerbates existing vulnerabilities, hindering access to healthcare, education, and employment opportunities. Conversely, countries providing more humane reception conditions, such as adequate housing, access to healthcare, and opportunities for integration into society, often see a more positive experience for asylum seekers while they wait for their claim to be processed. This humane approach aligns with international human rights standards and contributes to a more just and compassionate asylum system.

Finally, the issue of offshore processing, employed by some countries, represents a significant weakness, often resulting in human rights violations. This practice involves transferring asylum seekers to processing centers in other countries, often with significantly lower protection standards. This practice not only shirks national responsibility but also frequently leads to individuals being denied due process and facing increased risks of exploitation, abuse, and indefinite detention. In contrast, streamlining domestic procedures through improving efficiency and transparency, while respecting human rights, allows the same level of screening with vastly better outcomes for all involved. The contrasting approaches highlight the crucial need for a more unified and internationally-coordinated approach to addressing the challenges of refugee protection.

6.2 Best Practices

Effective refugee protection hinges on robust legal frameworks and efficient procedures. Countries like Canada, lauded for their relatively swift processing times and commitment to due process, often serve as models. Their emphasis on fair hearings and access to legal counsel ensures that asylum claims are thoroughly examined, minimizing the risk of erroneous decisions. This proactive approach not only protects vulnerable individuals but also enhances the overall legitimacy of the asylum system. Such transparency fosters public trust and encourages cooperation amongst stakeholders.

However, even the most well-intentioned systems grapple with limitations. Resource constraints, particularly in nations dealing with large influxes of asylum seekers, frequently lead to lengthy processing delays. Backlogs can cause significant hardship for applicants, creating uncertainty and delaying their access to essential services. Therefore, strategic resource allocation, coupled with innovative technologies that streamline administrative processes, becomes crucial. Investing in efficient digital systems for case management and data analysis can significantly mitigate these challenges.

A significant strength observed in several jurisdictions—including Sweden and Germany in Europe—is the integration of community-based support networks. These initiatives provide vital psychosocial services, language training, and employment assistance, helping refugees integrate into their new environments. Such holistic approaches are not merely humanitarian gestures; they are crucial for successful integration, promoting self-sufficiency and reducing the long-term strain on public resources. Empowering refugees to become active members of society contributes significantly to societal cohesion and overall well-being.

The importance of independent oversight mechanisms cannot be overstated. Independent bodies, such as national human rights institutions or specialized refugee tribunals, play a vital role in ensuring the accountability of government agencies and safeguarding against potential abuses. Their ability to review decisions, investigate complaints, and issue recommendations strengthens the integrity of the asylum process and protects against arbitrary decisions. This independent scrutiny safeguards the rights of asylum seekers and contributes to more equitable outcomes.

Protecting children is paramount. Many asylum systems demonstrate strengths in creating specialized pathways for unaccompanied minors and providing them with tailored protection and support. This involves prioritizing their safety, ensuring access to education and healthcare, and securing long-term placement in appropriate care settings. Robust child protection frameworks are not only ethically imperative but also contribute to the long-term well-being of young refugees, potentially helping them avoid exploitation and contribute positively to their communities.

Successful legal frameworks also emphasize the importance of international cooperation. Agreements and information-sharing mechanisms between nations can streamline the process, prevent duplication of effort, and avoid jurisdictional loopholes that could hinder access to protection. Such collaborative approaches enable a more coordinated and efficient response to refugee crises, reducing the burden on individual states and improving the overall effectiveness of global refugee protection.

Stronger emphasis should be placed on addressing the root causes of displacement. This means investing in conflict resolution, promoting good governance, and addressing issues like poverty and climate change that force people to flee their homes. While providing humanitarian assistance is essential, a long-term solution requires tackling the underlying problems that fuel displacement and create a more sustainable environment for those forced to leave their homes. This is a complex, multi-faceted approach requiring concerted efforts from international organizations and nation-states.

Furthermore, regular review and adaptation of asylum laws are critical. The evolving global landscape demands flexibility and responsiveness from legal frameworks. Regular assessments of the effectiveness and efficiency of existing procedures, guided by statistical data and qualitative feedback from stakeholders, ensure the continuous improvement of asylum systems and their capacity to adapt to changing circumstances. This dynamic approach will lead to more efficient procedures and improve the overall success rate of achieving durable solutions for refugees. The goal is never to achieve a perfectly static system but rather a continuously adapting, ever-improving process.

6.3 Areas for Improvement

Many asylum systems struggle with efficiency and fairness. Backlogs are commonplace, leading to protracted uncertainty and hardship for asylum seekers. Processing times often exceed reasonable limits, exacerbating stress and impacting access to essential services like healthcare and housing. These delays aren't merely administrative inconveniences; they represent a profound failure to provide timely protection to vulnerable individuals. Streamlining procedures, investing in adequate resources (staffing, technology, and training), and implementing clear timelines are crucial steps toward improvement. A concerted effort to reduce bureaucracy and enhance efficiency is paramount, ensuring that decisions are reached swiftly and fairly, without compromising due process.

A significant area needing attention is the consistency and predictability of asylum decisions. Inconsistencies across different jurisdictions and even within the same jurisdiction create a system prone to arbitrary outcomes. Such discrepancies undermine the rule of law and raise serious concerns about fairness and equality. Standardized criteria, clear guidelines for decision-making, and improved judicial oversight can significantly improve this. This includes providing more transparent reasons for decisions, allowing for effective appeals processes, and ensuring judges are properly trained in refugee law and human rights principles. Transparency enhances accountability and fosters greater trust in the system.

The quality of legal representation significantly influences asylum outcomes. Many asylum seekers lack access to competent legal counsel, placing them at a considerable disadvantage in navigating complex legal procedures. This inequality of access undermines the fairness of the asylum process. Ensuring that all asylum seekers have access to qualified legal representation, including pro bono services and legal aid programs, is fundamental for a just system. Further, exploring innovative approaches, such as providing standardized legal information materials, can improve understanding of the process and empower asylum seekers to better advocate for themselves.

Reception conditions for asylum seekers vary dramatically across jurisdictions, ranging from adequate provision of housing, food and healthcare to inadequate and even inhumane conditions. The treatment of asylum seekers during the asylum procedure forms a crucial indicator of a nation's commitment to human rights. Ensuring that all asylum seekers are housed in safe, humane, and appropriate accommodations with access to essential services is not only a moral imperative but also crucial for their physical and psychological well-being. Regular inspections of asylum reception centers should be conducted by independent bodies to maintain standards and promptly address any shortcomings.

International cooperation is essential to address the global refugee crisis effectively. The sharing of best practices, information, and resources across jurisdictions can dramatically improve the efficiency and fairness of asylum procedures. Collaborating on joint initiatives to address the root causes of displacement and promoting coordinated approaches to refugee resettlement are vital steps. Strengthening international legal frameworks and creating more robust mechanisms for accountability are also crucial steps to address global refugee issues, promoting a more unified, coherent, and efficient response. A truly effective system necessitates collaboration, not isolated national efforts.

The integration of asylum seekers into their new communities is often overlooked. Successful integration is not solely the responsibility of the asylum seeker; it requires a collaborative effort from host governments, civil society organizations and the wider community. Providing opportunities for language training, cultural orientation, and employment support contributes significantly to the well-being of asylum seekers and their successful integration. Promoting social inclusion and countering xenophobia through educational campaigns and community initiatives is vital to creating welcoming and supportive environments for newcomers. A successful integration reduces the social strain on communities and benefits both the asylum seekers and host countries. This process, while crucial, often receives inadequate attention. Finally, addressing the root causes of displacement is arguably the most critical long-term solution to the global refugee crisis. Investing in conflict prevention, promoting good governance, fostering sustainable development, and addressing issues such as poverty and inequality are vital to reducing the need for asylum. International cooperation is crucial in this regard, targeting the underlying factors that compel people to flee their homes and seek safety elsewhere. Tackling these root causes not only addresses the symptoms of displacement but offers long-term, sustainable solutions to the refugee issue. This approach proactively seeks to reduce the number of people needing protection, minimizing the pressure on already stretched asylum systems.

7 Conclusion: Future Directions

The preceding chapters have meticulously documented the complexities and inconsistencies inherent in global asylum procedures. A clear pattern emerges: the pursuit of effective refugee protection is consistently hampered by a lack of cohesive international cooperation, inconsistent national implementation of international law, and persistent human rights violations. This necessitates a comprehensive re-evaluation of the current framework, moving beyond mere analysis to actionable, impactful reforms.

Strengthening international cooperation is paramount. The current system, fragmented and often reactive, fails to adequately address the root causes of displacement—conflict, persecution, and climate change. A proactive, multilateral approach is needed, involving not only governments but also international organizations, NGOs, and even the private sector. This could involve collaborative efforts in conflict resolution, sustainable development initiatives in vulnerable regions, and coordinated resettlement programs that fairly distribute the burden among nations. Crucially, robust mechanisms for monitoring and accountability must be established, ensuring that commitments are met and transgressions are swiftly addressed. Funding for such initiatives needs substantial increase and must be committed by high-income nations based on their capacity.

One key area needing immediate attention is the harmonization of international refugee law. While the 1951 Refugee Convention and its 1967 Protocol provide a foundational framework, their interpretation and implementation vary wildly across jurisdictions. This lack of uniformity leads to inconsistencies in the recognition of refugee status and the provision of protection, creating loopholes exploited by states with restrictive asylum policies. A concerted effort is needed to clarify ambiguous provisions, establish consistent standards for determining refugee status, and develop comprehensive guidelines for the fair and efficient processing of asylum claims. The implementation of a universally applicable definition of a refugee could resolve many of the current ambiguities.

Furthermore, national asylum systems must be reformed to prioritize efficiency, fairness, and human dignity. This includes addressing the chronic problem of lengthy processing times, which often leave asylum seekers in limbo, vulnerable to exploitation and hardship. Investing in efficient administrative processes, providing adequate legal aid to asylum seekers, and ensuring access to fair and impartial judicial review are crucial steps. Reception conditions also require urgent improvement, ensuring that asylum seekers are housed in safe, humane environments with access to essential services, including healthcare, education, and psychosocial support. Such a change needs proper funding to guarantee it works effectively.

Ultimately, protecting refugee rights demands a fundamental shift in perspective. Refugees are not merely statistical figures or burdens on national resources; they are individuals fleeing persecution and seeking safety and opportunity. This inherent human dignity must be at the forefront of all policy decisions and actions. A more humane and compassionate approach, recognizing the inherent rights of asylum seekers and providing pathways to integration, is necessary. The adoption of this approach requires a change of social attitudes and government policies, requiring advocacy and awareness to ensure a society respects and cares for vulnerable people.

The journey towards a more just and equitable international refugee protection system will be long and challenging. However, by focusing on strengthening international cooperation, harmonizing legal frameworks, reforming national procedures, and prioritizing human dignity, the international community can move closer to fulfilling its moral and legal obligations to refugees. This is not simply a matter of legal compliance; it is a matter of human decency and global responsibility, a testament to humanity's ability to respond effectively and compassionately to the global refugee crisis. This requires a conscious, focused effort by all stakeholders involved in refugee protection. The alternative — continued inaction and indifference — is simply unacceptable. The time for decisive action is now. The future of refugee protection depends on it.

7.1 Recommendations for Reform

Streamlining asylum procedures is paramount. Lengthy processing times create undue hardship for applicants, exacerbating their vulnerability and delaying access to essential services. To remedy this, governments should invest in efficient administrative systems, leveraging technology where possible, and implementing clear timelines for each stage of the process. This includes providing adequate resources for staff training and interpreter services, crucial components often overlooked. Furthermore, proactive case management can significantly reduce backlogs and prevent unnecessary delays. This streamlined approach ensures a fairer and more timely resolution for asylum seekers, a key aspect of upholding their rights.

Clearer legal frameworks are essential. Ambiguity in legislation leads to inconsistent application and creates opportunities for discrimination. National laws must align explicitly with international refugee law, specifically the 1951 Refugee Convention and its 1967 Protocol, ensuring that all asylum claims are assessed against universally accepted standards. This includes defining key terms consistently and providing detailed procedures for each stage of the process, minimizing the potential for arbitrary decisions. Regular legal reviews and updates are necessary to adapt to evolving circumstances and jurisprudence, ensuring the legal framework remains relevant and effective. Transparency in legal processes is also critical, promoting accountability and building public trust.

Improving reception conditions is vital. Many asylum seekers endure inadequate living conditions, lacking access to basic necessities like shelter, food, and healthcare. This undermines their well-being and dignity, exacerbating the trauma they've already experienced. Governments should ensure that reception facilities meet minimum standards of safety, hygiene, and comfort, providing access to essential services. This includes dedicated healthcare facilities with mental health support, recognizing the unique psychological needs of asylum seekers. Moreover, programs fostering community integration and access to education and employment should be implemented to promote self-sufficiency and a sense of belonging. Addressing these fundamental needs demonstrates respect for human dignity and promotes a more compassionate approach to asylum.

Strengthening international cooperation is fundamental. The global refugee crisis necessitates a coordinated, multilateral response. International organizations, like UNHCR, should play a leading role in facilitating information sharing and promoting best practices. This includes standardizing asylum procedures where possible, improving data collection, and creating mechanisms for joint investigations into allegations of human rights violations. Governments should collaborate on burden-sharing initiatives, ensuring that responsibility for protecting refugees is not solely borne by a few nations. Effective coordination helps to manage refugee flows more effectively and prevents the exploitation of vulnerable populations. This collaborative approach is crucial for ensuring equitable access to protection and alleviating the pressure on individual states.

Addressing the root causes of displacement is imperative. While providing refuge is crucial, addressing the underlying conflicts and conditions that cause displacement is equally essential. This requires a multifaceted approach involving diplomatic efforts, humanitarian aid, and long-term development programs focused on promoting peace, stability, and economic opportunities in countries of origin. Investing in conflict resolution, strengthening governance, and promoting human rights are vital steps in reducing displacement and creating the conditions for voluntary return. A sustained effort to address the root causes is a fundamental aspect of comprehensive refugee protection, offering a long-term solution to the problem. Without addressing these issues, the cycle of displacement will continue.

Promoting integration and social inclusion is critical. Successful integration requires a multi-faceted approach, fostering social cohesion and enabling refugees to participate fully in their new societies. This requires language training, job skills development, and access to education. Governments should actively support initiatives fostering cultural understanding and bridging societal divides. Successful integration benefits both refugees and host communities, creating enriched, diverse societies. It's crucial to combat discrimination and xenophobia actively, creating a welcoming environment where refugees can build new lives. Long-term integration policies should foster self-reliance and meaningful participation in society, which is key to building inclusive and prosperous communities.

7.2 Strengthening International Cooperation

Effective international cooperation is paramount for a just and efficient global refugee protection system. The current fragmented approach, with each nation operating largely in isolation, leaves significant gaps and inconsistencies, often resulting in inadequate protection and the exploitation of vulnerable individuals. A coordinated, multilateral strategy is crucial. This requires not only shared legal frameworks and standards but also a commitment to collaborative action in areas like burden-sharing, data collection, and the development of comprehensive resettlement programs.

Strengthening international cooperation needs a multi-pronged approach. First, we must enhance the capacity of international organizations like UNHCR to effectively monitor asylum procedures globally and provide technical assistance to states with limited resources. This includes facilitating access to training, expertise, and funding for capacity building. Furthermore, strengthening the mandate and enforcement mechanisms of these organizations is crucial to holding states accountable for their obligations under international law. Without a robust monitoring and enforcement mechanism, international legal frameworks remain largely symbolic, failing to translate into real-world protection for refugees. Effective monitoring must be coupled with clear consequences for non-compliance.

Secondly, collaborative efforts are needed to address the root causes of displacement. This involves tackling conflict, poverty, and environmental degradation through coordinated international initiatives. Focusing solely on managing the consequences of displacement, while ignoring its underlying causes, creates a never-ending cycle of crisis. International cooperation must extend beyond emergency response to address long-term solutions, investing in sustainable development and conflict prevention in vulnerable regions. These efforts would not only reduce refugee flows but also improve the overall well-being of populations at risk, creating more stable and prosperous societies.

Improved data sharing and information management constitute another critical area for international collaboration. Accurate and consistent data on refugee populations, their needs, and their movements are essential for effective planning and resource allocation. This necessitates the development of standardized data collection protocols and the creation of secure platforms for sharing information among states and international organizations. Currently, the lack of reliable data often hinders effective responses, leading to misallocation of resources and inefficient planning.

Beyond data sharing, joint resettlement programs are vital. Burden-sharing among nations remains a persistent challenge, with a few countries bearing the disproportionate weight of hosting refugees. A more equitable distribution of responsibility requires a cooperative agreement where wealthier nations actively participate in resettlement schemes, ensuring a more fair and sustainable distribution of refugee populations. This demands financial contributions and tangible commitments to resettlement quotas that are both ambitious and realistically achievable. International cooperation here must transcend mere rhetoric and involve concrete commitments from wealthy states.

Moreover, concerted efforts should focus on enhancing the harmonization of asylum procedures. While respecting national sovereignty, we need more consistent standards and legal interpretations across jurisdictions. This reduces the potential for 'asylum shopping', where individuals seek asylum in countries with more lenient policies, and it avoids inconsistencies in protection levels. Harmonization can be achieved through the development of model laws, the sharing of best practices, and the establishment of mechanisms for resolving conflicts of jurisdiction. The aim is not to homogenize asylum procedures, but to create a system that provides similar levels of protection to all refugees, regardless of where they seek asylum.

Finally, bolstering legal frameworks and mechanisms for addressing human rights violations against refugees is crucial. This necessitates stronger international cooperation to ensure accountability for states that violate the rights of refugees, including the principle of non-refoulement. This can be achieved by creating effective mechanisms for reporting violations, independent investigations, and the imposition of targeted sanctions against individuals and states responsible for abuses. Strengthening international mechanisms and legal frameworks ensures that those perpetuating human rights violations against refugees are held accountable.

Ultimately, strengthening international cooperation requires a fundamental shift in mindset, moving away from a reactive, crisis-management approach to a proactive, preventative strategy. This shift demands a genuine commitment from all states to uphold their obligations under international law, cooperate in addressing the root causes of displacement, and share the responsibility for protecting vulnerable individuals. The well-being and future of countless refugees depend on it.

7.3 Protecting Refugee Rights

Effective refugee protection necessitates a multi-pronged strategy, demanding collaborative efforts from governments, international organizations, and civil society. International legal frameworks, such as the 1951 Refugee Convention and its 1967 Protocol, provide a crucial foundation, yet their implementation varies significantly across nations. Consistent application of the principle of non-refoulement—the prohibition of returning individuals to places where they face danger—is paramount, requiring robust monitoring mechanisms and accountability measures for state actors. This includes addressing situations where individuals are returned to countries where they face persecution, torture, or other human rights violations, regardless of the legality of their presence.

Strengthening national asylum systems is vital. This involves streamlining bureaucratic processes, ensuring access to legal aid and fair hearings, and establishing clear and transparent criteria for determining refugee status. Expeditious processing prevents prolonged uncertainty and suffering for asylum seekers. Equally important is ensuring access to adequate housing, healthcare, and education, promoting integration into host communities. Inadequate reception conditions are frequently a concern and must be improved to ensure dignified treatment and minimal psychological distress. In some jurisdictions, lengthy delays and backlogs add further hardship for those awaiting asylum decisions.

International cooperation is indispensable. Sharing responsibility for refugee resettlement through equitable burden-sharing agreements among countries with greater capacity is needed. This prevents undue strain on individual nations while providing better prospects for refugee integration and access to essential resources. Furthermore, joint efforts to address the root causes of displacement—conflict, persecution, and environmental disasters—are essential for long-term solutions. Addressing these underlying issues will decrease refugee flows and reduce the pressure on existing asylum systems, offering a more sustainable approach to the humanitarian crisis.

Protecting the rights of refugee children is critical. They are especially vulnerable to exploitation and abuse, thus requiring specific safeguards. This includes providing access to education, healthcare, and psychosocial support and safeguarding them from detention wherever possible. Children often face separation from their families, heightening their vulnerability. Family reunification should be prioritized, and their needs taken into account when determining asylum claims, creating a protective legal environment where they can thrive and integrate into their new communities.

Financial support for refugee protection is frequently insufficient. Increased and sustained funding for UNHCR and other humanitarian organizations is crucial. Resources must cover a wide range of needs, from providing shelter and basic necessities to ensuring adequate legal representation and facilitating integration efforts. Efficient and transparent use of funds is key to improving accountability and ensuring that aid reaches those who need it most. Donor countries have a vital responsibility to uphold their commitments and provide the necessary financial assistance to support effective refugee protection globally.

Beyond material support, protecting refugee rights demands a shift in societal attitudes and the dismantling of harmful prejudices. Combating xenophobia and discrimination through public awareness campaigns and education initiatives is key to creating inclusive societies where refugees feel welcome and safe. Building bridges of understanding between host communities and newcomers strengthens social cohesion and fosters mutual respect. Education plays a central role in fostering tolerance and dispelling myths and misconceptions about refugees, promoting a welcoming environment within host communities.

Ultimately, a comprehensive approach to refugee protection necessitates a convergence of legal reforms, international cooperation, and societal shifts. By focusing on these areas, governments and civil society organizations can create more humane and just asylum systems that safeguard the rights of those who have fled persecution and conflict. The success of such efforts rests on the collective commitment of all stakeholders to uphold the principles of international law and promote a more just and equitable world for refugees and asylum seekers. Failure to do so results in perpetuating cycles of violence and suffering.

www.ingramcontent.com/pod-product-compliance
Lightning Source LLC
LaVergne TN
LVHW022026200926
848481LV00007B/2562